Learning
Unlimited:
the home-based education case-files

by Roland Meighan

*with a foreword by Rupert Vansittart
('Lord Ashfordly' in ITV's 'Heartbeat')
and his wife, Emma Watson*

E

D1076598

Published 2001 by Educational Heretics Press
113 Arundel Drive, Bramcote Hills, Nottingham NG9 3FQ

British Cataloguing in Publication Data

Meighan, Roland
        Learning Unlimited: the home-based education case files
        1.Home schooling – Great Britain
        I.Title
        371'.042'0941

ISBN   1-900219-18-2

Design and production: Educational Heretics Press

Cover design by John Haxby, Edinburgh EH6 6QH

Printed by Esparto, Slack Lane, Derby

Foreword
by Rupert Vansittart
('Lord Ashfordly' in ITV's 'Heartbeat')
and his wife, Emma Watson

Upwards of 25,000 families home-educate their children in UK. Each family will have their own reasons for home-educating and each family will have its own methods of home-educating. But one thing they all do have in common. They have all taken the decision to step out of the main-stream.

And what a decision that is. The exhilaration of freedom, the thrill of determining for yourself how you and your family are going to live your lives, the taking back of responsibility.

Emotionally and intellectually your children bloom and blossom. Learning becomes fun, a journey of joy and fascination. Minds expand and the world of knowledge can be a friend once again. But, you have stepped out of the main-stream.

You must now be a threat to those who have not taken this decision. In one way or another they might go on the attack. (Emma and I were anonymously reported to the police for having the temerity to home-educate!) You may find yourself battling with your local education authority, though I must say ours has never been anything less than wholly supportive. You may find people you thought were friends suddenly being not quite the friends that they used to be. Or members of your family not being quite as familial as perhaps they once were.

None of this matters though. Because you are in the process of giving your children what is possibly the best start in life that children can have: a home education.

The case-files in Roland Meighan's excellent book will show you what the life of a home-educator can be. You will read of the doubts and fears, certainly. You will also read of the highs, of the empowerment, of the pleasure of happy children learning naturally, easily and without tears!

This book will both encourage and support. It can do no other. It is written by one of the most inspirational educators in the country; Dr. Roland Meighan.

Contents

Introduction

From 1977 onwards, and for about fifteen years, I was an educational double agent. Some of my time was spent in teacher education, preparing post-graduate students for a career in schools, and some of my time was spent researching and supporting families who chose to educate their children at home.

The contrast between school-based and home-based education has been likened to that between factory farming and the free-range option. A humane, flexible, personalised and democratic learning system - the next learning system - should utilize elements of both.

Since I have always argued for a more flexible, diverse and personalised learning system, I saw no necessary contradiction in the double agent role. But others, wedded to the orthodoxy of the mass coercive schooling system, are disturbed by this dual role.

Partly, this is due to the fact that home-based education tends to expose, rather starkly, the severe limitations of the schooling system and the damage it inflicts. This ranges from forcing the surrender of the influence of the family to be handed over to the tyranny of the peer group, to replacing the constructive approach of most families seeking to create a better world, with the fatalistic 'toughen them up for real life in the nasty competitive world' philosophy.

These are only two of the criticisms to be found. For his Ph.D research, Nigel Wright catalogued 291 separate negative criticisms to be found in the literature. (The book he wrote, derived from his Ph.D research is entitled *Assessing Radical Education*, 1989, Open University Press.)

All the case-files in this book are based on true incidents. All names and most locations have been changed to avoid any possible embarrassment, with the exception of the Appendix.

The author has permitted himself some poetic licence in the files, over such things as the actual dialogue and the exact sequence of events.

In an earlier book, Flexischooling (1988), I paid unsponsored tribute to the new technology - the Amstrad 8256 Word Processor. In times of continuous change, we all have to relearn, and so this time I need to acknowledge (unsponsored) that this book was 'written' by voice using the *Dragondictate Naturally Speaking* programme on an Elonex PC.

Roland Meighan

Case-file one

The road crossing

Mary ran into the kitchen, straight into the arms of her mother.
"Alan is in hospital!" she cried.
"Is he all right? What has happened?"
"He was hit by a car and he has hurt his arms and legs."
"When did this happen?"
"He was crossing the main road on his way to school."

It was Saturday morning. Mary's father, Dan, called the meeting to order. All six families with children in the cul-de-sac were represented by one or more parents.
"We have all written to the local authority about the need for a crossing on the main road for children going to school. We warned them that one day there would be a bad accident. Well, yesterday it happened. What are we going to do about it? I have a suggestion, but has anyone else got any ideas?"
"We could write again."
"We could organise a petition."
"We could write to our M.P."
"We could write to the newspapers."
"What is your idea, Dan?"
"I propose we 'go on strike', and do not send our children to school until a safe crossing is in place."
"But won't our children lose track of what is going on at school?"
"We would co-operate with the school - I'm sure they will support us - so that we can do similar work at home. They may even send a teacher over to help us, from time to time."

A long and earnest discussion followed. But one contribution proved to be decisive. One parent said that the next child to be hit by car might not be so lucky. *"We might have a funeral on our hands,"* she said.

"Why not telephone the head teacher and see what she has to say about the idea?" said one parent. Dan said that he would do that right away. Sarah suggested that now was a good time for her to make some tea and coffee and get some biscuits, so that everyone could have a break.

Dan phoned the head teacher and explained the situation. The teachers at the school would be sympathetic, said the head teacher, after a little thought. She agreed to give the families any support that she could provide, and that the law allowed.

Armed with this information, the meeting resolved to go ahead with their strike and conduct their 'schools at home' for the time being. Dan raised another issue:
"What do people feel about talking to the press, or being interviewed on radio, or even television?"
Quite a lively discussion followed. Some people were wary of the media and the way they could distort what you tell them and the ideas you represent. On the other hand, publicity would help the cause of getting a safe crossing. In the end, they all agreed they must co-operate with the media, but give heavy stress to the main points. These were that they had no dispute with the school - the reason for their strike was the lack of a safe crossing. The activity of the families in educating their children at home was a temporary expedient until it was safe for their children to travel to school.

On the Sunday evening before the strike was due to start, Dan, Sarah, and their three children, Stan aged 10, Mary aged 8, and Tom aged 6 had a family meeting. They had been talking all day about what they would do in their 'school at home'. Now they needed to make some plans. Dan would be at work but he would be involved in the evenings and at the weekends. Stan declared,
"I think we should meet at 9:00 around the table, ready to start."
Sarah groaned inwardly. She had been hoping for a more relaxed start to the proceedings – 9.30 or thereabouts.

"Until we get some information about lessons from the school, we can all do a topic," said Mary.
"Do you mean a topic each, or one we do together?" asked Stan.

"We could do both," said Mary.
"Tom is very tired now," said Sarah, *"so let's decide on topics tomorrow morning."*

The Monday morning meeting began promptly at 9:00.
"I have a topic," said Tom, *"I want to learn more about birds."*
"I want to learn about canals," said Mary.
"My topic will be magicians," said Stan, *"I want to find out how they do those tricks and illusions."*
"Have we got a topic for us to do together?" asked Sarah. Nobody had any suggestions.
"I have always wanted to to find out more about festivals," said Sarah. *"Why do we have holly and mistletoe at Christmas, and eggs and bunnies at Easter, and what is the 'festival of light' that some people celebrate?"*
Well, everybody thought that might be interesting to investigate.

The discussion continued. They decided that they would need to visit the library. They would need to go to the museum, and the information centre. They might need to find a local member of the magic circle and to contact the local bird-watching society. They would need to go to the newsagent to look for any magazines related to their topics. They would need to check the radio and television schedules to see if there were any programmes linked to their topics. They were going to be busy.

The school took a little time to get information together to help the families. By that time all the families were busy researching and exchanging ideas for their various investigations. Somehow, they would have to put aside some time to do the kind of things the school had in mind.

Soon they had gained all they could about the topics from the books and materials in the house, so they visited their local library.   The librarian was very helpful.   First of all she explained that because the family was being educated at home, even on a temporary basis, they would be able to take out up to 15 books each.   Then, she informed them that there was an organisation for people educating at home, called *Education Otherwise*. This organisation had gathered plenty of information and advice for anyone starting to educate at home. A small group of local home-educating families met every Tuesday afternoon in the meeting room that was part of the library. They could meet this group, if they wanted. In the meantime, if anyone needed help with finding books for their topics, they needed only to ask.

When Dan came home each evening, he was surrounded by his children wanting to show him what they had been doing and to pick his brains about their investigations. This was quite a contrast to past exchanges, which had followed this pattern:
"What did you do at school today?"
"Oh, some Maths, some English, that kind of thing."

Weeks went by. The family learnt how to spend a little time doing the school work sent to them by the teachers and a lot more time pursuing their own researches. They learnt how to co-operate with the other families and to find out about their investigations. The families organised things to do together. They organised their first outing, and then their second and then their third. They visited a park where there was a zoo, a small fun fair, a lake with plenty of bird life, so there was plenty for everyone to do and plenty of things to learn. They found out more about *Education Otherwise*. They found out that up to one third of home-educating families had a teacher as one of the parents, and that plenty of famous people had been home-educated. They had a meeting with the local group.

The newspaper arrived. There was an announcement. The local council had finally agreed to establish a crossing, on the main road, so the children can travel safely to school. Then, a letter arrived from the school. Now that there was a safe crossing, the teachers were looking forward to having the children attend school again. The school was pleased that the action of the parents, their 'strike', had had a positive effect. The news was not well received. It was Wednesday, and the school was expecting them to return on the Monday. There would be only a few more days of their 'school at home'.

Dan called the meeting of the striking families to order.
"I thought you all ought to know that this family has decided that its 'school at home' is just too successful to finish. So we are going to become a home educating family from now on. If any other families want to join us, they would be most welcome."

Case-file two

The prospective teacher

Susan was driving into the countryside. She had taken up the invitation made by her tutor to spend a day with a family educating their children at home. She wondered how useful this would be in preparing her to become a teacher, but it was bound to be interesting anyway.

She found the village, and then the street and then the house, and parked the car outside. By the time she was out of the car, one of the family was already coming down the drive to meet her. *"You must be Susan - come in and meet everybody."*

It was coffee time, and before long, it she had a mug of steaming coffee in one hand and a homemade piece of cake in the other. Soon, she felt very relaxed. Everyone seemed pleased to see her. The mother, Gwen, said, *"we tend to follow a pattern where everybody does their own projects between breakfast and coffee break."*

"At coffee break we discuss whether we will be doing any things together, or in pairs, or carry on doing our own individual tasks, or whatever pattern works for everybody's satisfaction. It is an informal review and planning meeting, although our main planning meeting usually takes place Sunday late afternoon or early evening."

Everyone was quite interested in why she wanted to be a teacher, and how the course was developing. They knew she was in a group that had adopted an unusual approach.

Susan explained that the group had taken up the invitation to work as a learning co-operative. This meant that they planned their own course, and worked out how to teach and learn it. They had devised their own programme and agreed amongst themselves who would take responsibility for particular sessions. This allowed them to go away and research a particular topic and devise ways in which the group might learn it.

One of the children said, *"That sounds very much like the way we work here in our family."* Susan agreed. The way the learning co-operative worked at the university and the family's 'plan, do and review' approach, had a lot in common.

She learnt that they were four children in the family. The eldest was Angela, now 15 years old, who had been to school for short time when aged 5, but had found it an unhappy experience. Jane was 14, and she had been to school for short time, but had found it a limiting and depressing time.

The parents, Gwen and Bill, had grown tired of taking two unhappy children to school, day after day, and had decided to try home-based education instead. It was a decision they had never regretted. Paul was now 13, and he had never been to school. David was 10, and he had never been to school either.

If either ever wanted to try school, they could, of course, do so. But learning at home was too absorbing and too interesting to give up. Friends who called round after school kept them informed about life at school and it did not sound appealing.

Over coffee they discussed how Susan would spend her day. Between coffee break and lunch she would be with the children and again after lunch. After the afternoon tea break she would spend time with the parents. After that, she would set off for home.

Well, she ended up having a very exciting day. At the end of it, she felt tired but exhilarated. As she was driving home she began to reflect on the events of the day.

She thought first of all about the lunch. Almost everything on the table had been grown in the garden. The family was almost self-sufficient in food and all the family members seemed very knowledgeable and capable both in the garden and in the plastic covered greenhouse.

When she had been shown around the house, she also learnt that the children were pretty capable builders. They showed her where they had installed central heating, replaced a rotten roof, built new walls, and converted a derelict out-house into a workshop. Bill was a builder by trade, and he had passed on his skills to his children.

Then they had shown her the car. It was an old Morris Minor. Recently they had stripped the car down to its last nut and bolt. Then they had rebuilt it and got it through its MOT test. The two girls have been working on the car, giving it a service and changing its oil, when she arrived at coffee time.

She reflected that this was outside her own present range of competence. Nor could she think of any of the females in her circle who had car mechanic skills.

She felt quite dazzled by all the things she had seen. The boys had shown her their beehives and explained how they had learnt to become bee-keepers. Later, she had had some of the honey on her bread. One of the children had baked the bread.

Two of the children were interested in making clothes. They had collected bits of sheep wool off barbed wire fences, and learnt how to spin it on old spinning wheel. They had learnt how to dye the wool and then how to knit it into garments.

The children all had their own bank accounts. From time to time, Bill would put in an estimate for a job and the whole family would be involved as workers. Then the money would be divided up amongst the family members.

From time to time the children would also earn money with such activities as selling honey, selling bread and cakes, and doing decorating and minor building tasks for friends and neighbours.

When Susan got home to her flat, she set about getting the evening meal - nothing was home-grown, she reflected ruefully. Afterwards, she would set about writing her report for the group on her day spent with a home-educating family. What was she going to say?

She began her report.

"It is supposed that I have one of the best forms of education that money can buy. I was awarded a first-class honours degree at Oxford University. But the children in this family made me feel rather poorly educated. They had a range of skills and competencies that I just could not match.

"Part of my degree is in politics and I did a special study on pressure and interest groups. The members of the family were interested in my work. They turned out to be members of several local groups, such as Friends of the Earth, Greenpeace, the Beekeepers Association and so on. The understanding of pressure and interest groups was practical. My understanding was, for the most part, theoretical.

"I think I'm going to have to reconsider completely my ideas about education, and what it means to be educated."

Case-file three

The seminar

The head teacher spoke. *"These home educating parents must be very arrogant to think they know better than the professionals."*
The tutor replied, *"You have to remember that as many as a third of home educating parents are teachers anyway."*
Another member of the seminar, a deputy head teacher, joined in. *"I would quite like to meet some of the home educating parents and talk with them about their experiences."*
Other members of the group, gave murmurs of approval. The group was part of the part-time Masters Degree in Education course at the University and was made up of head teachers, deputy head teachers, and other senior members of the teaching profession from the locality. The tutor agreed to invite some home-educating parents to the next seminar in a weeks time.

The following week, the parents arrived early and began to talk among themselves. They had all met each other at meetings of their home education support group. Elizabeth was a former teacher who was educating her three children at home. Nigel was a self-employed landscape-gardener who was able to find some time to help his wife out with their home educating programme. Elaine was a free-lance journalist and a single parent who had decided in favour of home-based education for her two children. The three were busy speculating that the first question would be about - socialisation.

The members of the seminar group began to arrive. Then the tutor arrived and the meeting started. He welcomed the parents and introduced the members of the seminar group. He knew all the home-educating parents since he was part of the local home-educating support group. So he introduced them briefly, and then asked them to say a few words about their situation.

Sure enough, the first question asked was about socialisation.

"Do you feel your children are missing out on the social life of school?"

Elizabeth gave her response: *"I see missing out on the social life of school as one of the main reasons for educating at home. I cannot remember my daughter doing anything mean-spirited until she went to school, where she began to learn some unpleasant habits."*

Nigel joined in. *"If the question of socialisation is the first one that occurs to you, you will understand that is also the first question that occurs to any parent contemplating home-based education. So families build into their learning programmes all sorts of opportunities for social contact."*

The tutor asked Elaine if she wanted to make any comment. She took the opportunity to say: *"The research shows quite clearly that the children who are educated at home usually develop more social skills and more social maturity than their friends at school. Whilst the social experience of children at school is confined to a group of similar age and equal immaturity, home educated children are mixing with people of all ages as they go about their learning in the community."*

The next question was posed by a head teacher in that confident manner of people thinking there would be no answer to the point being made. *"Even though school is far from perfect, why aren't you trying to improve the system from within, rather than seeking to give your children a better deal than everybody else?"*

Nigel spoke first. *"I think John Holt gave an interesting answer to this question in one of his books. He said that the majority of the world's children would feed today on a bowl of rice. The logic of your argument is that we should all feed our children on a bowl of rice, rather than trying to give them a better deal than everyone else. As they learnt to starve like everybody else, we would spend our time trying to reform the world's economic systems. Nobody I know seems to think that is a good idea."*

"For most of my working life, I have been trying in my own small way, to introduce reforms into the schools in which I've worked," said Elizabeth. *"Any success is temporary and the*

system soon reverts to its regimental and domination-riddled practices. Only cosmetic change is permitted; radical change is resisted. So, trying to reform the system from within, is futile."

Elaine added her thoughts, *"It's not that school is just imperfect, it is obsolete and counter-productive, and its main achievement is to give children a whole series of bad habits - bad intellectual, social, moral, emotional, and political habits. In other words, it does damage to children. Some children are badly damaged, most are moderately damaged, and a few slightly damaged. I came to see that compulsory, coercive, mass schooling is also an abuse of at least three human rights."*

Nigel added, *"Illich made a distinction between institutions that were coercive and those that were convivial. An army is coercive and so is a prison, whereas a pub is convivial and so is a public library. My experience is that schools almost always are coercive institutions and not convivial ones."*

One of the seminar group members protested, *"I try my best to make my classrooms convivial, and I know some of my colleagues try to do the same. Aren't you being rather hard on the teaching profession?"*

Elizabeth responded, *"I, too, try to make my classrooms convivial but I always felt I was swimming against the tide. It is not so much teachers as the system. As Everett Reimer observed, some true educational experiences are bound to occur in schools. They occur, however, despite school and not because of it."*

One of the members of the seminar group turned to the tutor. *"Do you think it is impossible to run a convivial school?"* The tutor replied, *"Not impossible but highly unlikely. Sudbury Valley school in the USA is a convivial school. It has no curriculum and no timetable until the learners decided to create them. The nearest we have to such a school is Summerhill and the government has been trying to close it down. But, now that I have the floor, I am going to suggest we take a break for refreshments."*

It was a longer coffee break than usual. The conversation was animated and nobody seemed to want to stop. Eventually, the tutor asked if everybody was ready to resume. There was no dissent, so people return to their places around the table. But the mood seemed to have changed. The professionals now seemed to be less interested in asserting their status, and more interested in listening to the parents.

The second session began with a new question. *"I was quite impressed with your knowledge of the educational literature. I don't know the books you mentioned and I would like to jot some details down."* The tutor suggested, *"Why don't we all mention a book on education that has influenced us and say a few words about it?"* There were nods of approval.

Nigel started. *"The book by Illich is called 'De-schooling Society'. In it he argues that mass schooling has been imposed to produce a population that will conform to the needs of business, for a steady stream of consumers. To do this, young children who are full of inquiry, asking on average 30 questions an hour, have to be processed to become dependent on others to tell them what to think."*

Elaine joined in. *"John Holt wrote ten books altogether. His first one, 'How Children Fail', really shocked me. It describes how the classroom is a hostile learning environment for children. So, they devise a series of defensive strategies to avoid humiliation. In the end, devising and using the strategies takes over from inquiry and thinking."*

It was Elizabeth's turn. *"A book that really make me think was Goodman's 'Compulsory Mis-education'. But there is a recent book by a former British teacher, Chris Shute, 'Compulsory Schooling Disease', that shows how a steady diet of imposed rules, routines and regimentation creates the slave mentality."*

The discussion continued as some of the professionals mentioned books that they had found of interest, often read some time ago during their training. Eventually, the tutor had to draw the proceedings to close. *"It might be possible for anybody interested to visit one of the families that are home-educating."* But the course members were already on to that one. *"Yes, we've already been fixing up visits during the coffee break!"*

Case-file four

The leaflet

Jean made for the shortest queue in the supermarket. She checked - daughter Ann was close at hand, but where was her son Ben?
"Can you see Ben?"
"He's over there talking to the lady in the yellow T-shirt and blue jeans," said Ann.
"What is he doing?"
"I think she was asking him about home-based education."
They both groaned.

Eventually, Jean, Ann and Ben settled themselves and the shopping in the car. Ben explained that the woman in the supermarket had asked him why he was not school. They all groaned.

"Don't tell me," said Ann, *"she didn't know that you can be educated at home if you choose to."*
They could all recite the all-too-familiar sequence of questions:
"Aren't you at school today?"
"But you have to go to school!"
"I didn't know it was legal to educate at home - are you sure?"
"But what about your friends, and what about socialisation?"
"Is your mother a trained teacher then?"
There was always shock at the answer that she was not a trained teacher and, indeed, did not have to be.

"Well," said Jean, *"you remember what that researcher from the University said at our conference last month - when you decide on home-based education, you not only take on board responsibility for your own education, but for the re-education of most of the world, because many people are misinformed, or ignorant of the law, or confused, or schooled into conformity and loss of imagination."*

Ben said that he did not understand why people had such a rosy picture of school. He had read in the paper about a survey that showed that adults were willing to continue learning throughout life provided that it was in a convivial setting such as home, or work, or a pub. But they did not want a coercive, school-type setting.

"They say that it never did me any harm!" said Ann, *"It would be a bit rude to say what I was thinking, which is you're not standing where I'm standing, because if you were, the harm done is obvious.   You cannot think very clearly and you are misinformed."*

"I came across a quotation from Tom Paine, the 'Rights of Man' writer, which said, 'A long habit of not thinking a thing wrong gives it a superficial appearance of being right.' I think that has something to do with it."

"I think we should produce a checklist of questions and answers," Ben said, *"Then when anyone stops us, we can just hand over the sheet and ask them to read it."*
"What a good idea," said Jean, *"but with our computer we can do better than a checklist, we could design and produce a leaflet.   With our colour printer, we could make it look quite smart."*

The idea began to excite all three of them. They would ask Tom what he thought of the idea when they got home. They could make this the next family project. They could start planning it later today.

But during the drive home, they were planning it anyway. They agreed that there should be a brief section on the law and home-based education. They would need another section on how they as a family saw education. Then there could be another section on how they went about planning their programmes of study. They could be some account of modern learning ideas - learning styles, multiple intelligences, new research on the brain and learning - that sort of thing. There could be mention of some useful web-sites so that people could get further information.

When they got home, Tom was already there.

"Dad, we've had an idea!" Ann and Ben burst out together, and went on to explain the idea so far. They wanted to know what he thought of it. Well, he thought it was brilliant.

He added another idea. He thought that one section should be a little light-hearted, perhaps quoting that joke about home-based education. It was the one that went:
"Question: How does a home educating family change a light bulb?
Answer: first, they get three books on electricity out of the library. Next they make models of light bulbs, read a biography of Thomas Edison, and act out a scene from his life.
After that, everyone studies the history of lighting methods, ending up with dipping their own candles. Later, everyone takes a trip to the shop where they compare types of light bulb as well as prices and they work out how much change they'll get if they buy two bulbs with a five pound note.

"On the way home, the discussion develops over the history of money, and also about the life of Wellington, because his picture was on the note. Finally, after building a home-made ladder out of branches dragged from the woods, the new light bulb is put in place."

Ben remarked, *"The only problem including this story, is if their schooling has not only dulled a particular reader's mind, but also their sense of humour."*

Jean got out the file on home-based education. It was a very thick file with lots of newspaper cuttings and information sheets. *"We may get some ideas from looking through this file. Here is a list of famous people who were educated at home. There are seventeen presidents of United States, Yehudi Menuhin the violinist, Thomas Edison, Agatha Christie, Margaret Mead - the anthropologist, the Queen, and many others. There was also that family in the film, 'The Sound of Music', the Von Trapp family. Funnily enough, lots of people who like that film forget that it was all about a home-educating family, and that later, Hitler and the Nazis made home-based education illegal because they wanted a highly conformist and regimental population."*

Next day, they all set to work on ideas for the leaflet. The first task, they decided, was to agree a statement of their aims and methods. Eventually, they agreed on the following statement:

In our 'free range' education at home, we set out to:
- learn how to learn and ask questions,
- learn creatively in our own personal style,
- learn what we are interested in,
- learn about the subject for as long as we like,
- learn by doing things not just by sitting all day,
- learn at our own individual pace and at our own level,
- learn to mix with different people of all ages,
- learn computers whenever we like,
- sing, dance and listen to music whenever we feel the need,
- go to the library whenever we need to,
- go on outings whenever we think it is desirable.

We do not try to copy the 'battery hen' approach to learning of the school system.

"We could mention some of the research in a brief section," said Ann, *"even if it is only to point out that children educated at home are, on average, two years ahead of those in school, and can be up to ten years ahead."*

Jean wanted to say something about multiple intelligences. They agreed to indulge her with the following statement:

Our learning is guided by the natural curriculum and its catalogue curriculum approach and not restricted by the national curriculum. We can study anything which interests us and in a real-life setting. We learn subjects which develop all of our intelligences in a creative and flexible way. This is the sort of thinking which will be needed in the future. The intelligences we seek to develop are those identified by Howard Gardner - logical and mathematical, verbal and linguistic, design and spatial, bodily and kinaesthetic, artistic, interpersonal, intra-personal, and naturalistic.

"We can put in a web-site reference for those who want to look up details of these various intelligences," said Ben.

Work continued throughout the day, and gradually, quite a smart looking leaflet began to take shape on the computer. When Tom came home from work, they were able to present him with a printed draft version. He was very impressed.

"I would like to see a rash of these leaflets appear all over the land, as family after family declared their own educational vision," he declared.

Case-file five

The kilt

The telephone rang. The woman on the other end spoke with a Scottish accent. She had been given my name as somebody who might be able to help with advice about home-based education. She had two problems. The first was how to deal with the local education authority, since their officers had sent a most unhelpful letter and wanted a meeting to lay down their terms. The second problem was how to go about organising a satisfactory home-based education programme.

She explained that she would rather not talk about their situation over the phone. The family lived about half an hour's drive away, so would it be possible for me to visit them? They would pay any expenses involved. I warmed to her - most people seemed to forget all about costs, whether it was costs of postage, costs of the telephone calls, cost of travel, or costs of time.

I arrived at their house to find that the whole family was assembled in Highland dress. There was the father Angus, the mother Heather, the elder son Duncan, the daughter Jean, and the younger son Jamie. Angus spoke first. *"Looking at your family name,"* he said, *"your forefathers came from somewhere south of Inverness."*

"So I understand," I said, *"but I was born and bred in England, in the Midlands, around Birmingham, so I've never worn a kilt."*
"Well," said Angus, *"you can try one on later if you'd like to. It doesn't worry you that we wear Highland dress?"*
"No," I replied, *"I think it looks rather splendid."*
"Well it really bothers the local schools, and the local authority."
And so I heard the full story. When the family arrived in the Midlands a few months ago, because of a job opportunity that Angus had taken, they approached a local secondary school on

behalf of the three children. They explained that they were proud of their Highland heritage, and would like to attend the school in Highland dress. The head teacher saw no problem. After all, they had learned to live with turbans and other dress variations in the school.

But within a couple of weeks, they had received a letter from the head teacher asking them to refrain from attending in kilts, because it was having a disruptive effect on the school. So the family went to see the head teacher who was clearly embarrassed to report that the children in the school were constantly disrupting lessons with an endless stream of jokes and comments about the Highland dress of the children. The teachers had been unable to stem the flow of verbal and other disruptions.

The family decided to approach another school. They explained that they were proud of their Highland heritage, and would like to attend the school in Highland dress. They explained what had gone on at the first school. The second head teacher saw no problem. After all they had learned to live with turbans, and girls in trousers and other dress variations.

But within a couple of weeks, they had received a letter from the second head teacher asking them to refrain from attending in kilts, because it was having a disruptive effect on the school. Again, the family went to see the head teacher who was clearly embarrassed to report that the children in the school were constantly disrupting lessons with an endless stream of jokes and comments about the Highland dress of the children. Again, the teachers had been unable to stem the flow of verbal and other disruptions.

The family decided to approach a third school. They explained that they were proud of their Highland heritage, and would like to attend the school in Highland dress. They explained what had gone on at the previous two schools. The head teacher was convinced that there would be no problem in his school. After all, they had learned to live with turbans and girls in trousers and other dress variations.

But within a couple of weeks, they had received a letter from the head teacher asking them to refrain from attending in kilts, because it was having a disruptive effect on the school. Once again, the family went to see the head teacher who was clearly embarrassed to report that the children in the school were constantly disrupting lessons with an endless stream of jokes and comments about the Highland dress of the children.   His teachers had been unable to stem the flow of verbal and other disruptions.

The family decided that enough was enough.   They would exercise their right to transfer to home-based education instead. They had already done their research. They had contacted *Education Otherwise* and had been given some local contacts. They had made contact with the local volunteer co-ordinator and then gone on to meet some local families who were home educating.

"How did the children of the home-educating families react to your Highland dress?"
"Just as you did," said Duncan, *"they said it looked rather splendid."*
"This does not come as a surprise," I said, *" because there is plenty of research to show that home-based educated children tend to be more emotionally mature, and more socially skilled, and more socially mature than their schooled counterparts. Schooled children are on average two years more immature – it is the institution of school and the way it fosters the tyranny of the peer group that holds them back."*

Heather spoke. *"The research you quote would also explain the difficulties children from England find when they go to local schools in the Highlands of Scotland. Their English ways of behaving, dressing and speaking, receive the same kind of treatment that our children have had here."*

Then we set to work. They showed me the letter from the local education authority. We went through it and explained all the legal errors that the local authority were making. Heather wrote down all the legal precedents.

The family was particularly concerned that the local authority officials thought that they could dictate the content and methods of the home education programme. I explained that a lengthy court case had established the right of the family to devise its own educational approach.

We talked about ideas for their programme of home-based education, but they had already assembled plenty of ideas of their own, and through talking with other home educating families. They already had arrangements to meet with some of these families, sometimes to do things together.

We had a meal together and then I began to say my goodbyes. Angus said, *"Thank you for coming and giving us such good information. I shall now enjoy meeting the local education authority official and putting him right on a few matters!"*

A week later the telephone rang. It was Heather, and she gave a graphic description of the meeting with the official. Apparently Angus had made sure his ceremonial dagger was at hand. When the official started to repeat the errors of the letter, Angus picked up his dagger and began to use it to give emphasis to the points of law they had checked out.

"The poor man seem to be quite hypnotised by the dagger, and his eyes followed every circular movement and dabbing movement it made. I think Angus began to play him like a fish on a fishing line. Anyway, all his objections were withdrawn one by one, and he seemed quite glad to get to the door, say his goodbyes and depart. To his credit, he did wish us all the best of luck.

"We have already found that switching to home-based education is a lucky break and we are all benefiting from it. The other home-educating families are very interested in our life and culture in the Highlands. Some want to do a project on it and use us as resources!"

Case-file six

The court case

The group of trainee teachers assembled for their Friday morning session. The student appointed to be chair for the morning called the meeting to order. The tutor raised his hand and was invited to speak.

"I need to give my apologies - I will not be able to attend next week's meetings. This is because I'm appearing as an expert witness, in Worcester, in an education case."

Yvonne, the student in the chair for the morning, said, *"This sounds intriguing, I think we would all like to have some information about this event."*

The tutor explained that a home-educating family was appealing against a school attendance order. The issue at stake was not whether home-based education itself was legitimate because the local authority had conceded that this was a legal option.

But the local educational authority was trying to insist that the family should educate in the way its officials prescribed. The family was claiming it had a right to devise its own programme of studies. It wanted to adopt the autonomous approach to education where the learners would manage their own curriculum, sometimes as individuals and sometimes in co-operation with other members of the family, and sometimes in co-operation with people outside the family. The officials wanted the family to study set subjects, with set textbooks, doing the tests they specified and having regular timetables. In other words they wanted home-based education to be a replica of school-based education, matching the approaches in the local schools. This would be an important test case.

This trainee teacher group operated in a somewhat similar way to the family. When they first met, the tutor had offered them three ways of running the course, the first being the familiar teacher-taught course, the second was an individualised course with tutorials, and the third a learning co-operative where the members of the group devised and managed their own course. After much debate and heart-searching, the group had somewhat nervously opted to try the third approach. But by now, they had developed confidence in their ability to trust and use their own intelligence and revive their dormant powers of co-operation, and they had few regrets about their unorthodoxy.

When it was time for the coffee break, the group members began to discuss the forthcoming court case. They realised this was a unique situation. One or two of the members said they would like to attend the court case. They were not alone, and in the end everyone voted to postpone their planned sessions for next week so that they could attend the court hearing. Enough members of the group had cars for everyone to get a lift. The tutor briefed them about where the court was situated and the time of the hearing.

When the court hearing began, all the members of the trainee teacher group were present in the visitors' gallery. It was a Crown Court hearing. The judge opened the proceedings and the barrister representing the local education authority made his opening statement. The barrister representing the family responded.

Then the proceedings began in earnest with the expert witnesses appearing in the witness box to be questioned and then cross-examined. The group witnessed the unusual sight of their tutor in the witness box for two hours or more being cross-examined by an aggressive barrister.

During the lunch break the group discussed the events of the morning. One member, Jenny, said, *"I have been making detailed notes of the proceedings, and I noticed others doing the same."*
"We were not the only ones," said another, *"the press box was packed with journalists from local and national newspapers, also making plenty of notes."*
Jenny said, *"I think we could make a simulation about this case for use in our classrooms. We could use it for one or two purposes. One would be to develop the idea of rival versions of*

education, and the other as an introduction to the British legal system."

Four members of the group were particularly keen on this idea. They knew that their tutor would help out with any background material that they needed. One of the group had been looking into the ways of making simulations and they knew that if they needed any more guidance on how to devise this kind of simulation, they could obtain it.

"It is time for the afternoon session," said one of the group. *"Does anyone know what will happen this afternoon?"*

"The family will be calling a well-known educational psychologist," said another member. *"This guy appeared as a witness in the famous Lady Chatterley case."*

"How do you know that?"

"Well, I have a particular interest in the law, and I managed to have a few words with the Clerk of the Court. The family has pretty strong line-up - their barrister is Lord Tony Gifford who is a top lawyer and a Q.C."

Two days later the hearing was over. The students had had an exciting time following the case and had debated the issues long and hard. They had all come to the conclusion that the family was in the right, and that the officials of the Local Authority were wrong. But they had a personal stake in this. As one member said, *"If the court finds that they are not permitted to manage their own education, then our learning co-operative approach could be put in question. We could be told that there is only one right way to do teacher education by having a set curriculum, and a prescribed subject matter, undertaken by formal instruction."*

(In fact, this did turnout to be a forecast. When the government decided to organise teacher education from London a few years later, they did indeed, prescribe their 'One Right Way'.)

But everyone would have to wait for the final judgment. The judge had decided to take time out before giving what proved to be a lengthy and detailed verdict.

But the working group on the simulation decided that they would devise the simulation in such a way that the pupils using it would not know the verdict, so that they would have to judge the issue as best they could, on the evidence and the way they played out the simulation.

The eventual judgement was long and complex, but in general, it vindicated the family. The judge decreed that there was more than one valid way to go about education. The autonomous approach to education, that the family preferred, was upheld as a viable approach. The family had been making a success of such an approach and the girls, who had now just passed the age of sixteen, were applauded as good examples:
"They are mature, confident and at ease in all sorts of company. They are lively-minded, have a good general knowledge and are intellectually athletic ... In their case, their education – in its own field – has proved and is proving, a marked success." (from Harrison v. Stevenson, 1981)

The local education authority was given a somewhat 'soft landing'. There was plenty of understanding and forgiveness for their unsympathetic behaviour, but not much allowance for the pain and distress they had caused, to say nothing of the waste of a large sum of taxpayers' money used up in taking this one family to court.

Case-file seven

The cliff-top picnic

Lt. Col. Baden Driscol (retired) put on his light wind-proof coat, his flat cap and picked up his walking stick. He was about to set off on his late morning walk across the field and along the cliff top. The weather was warm and sunny and there was a steady cool breeze.

He left the house with his dog Scout and set off at a brisk pace. Soon they reached the cliff top and climbed over the stile. Scout ran on ahead and disappeared by some bushes along the path. When Baden reached the place where Scout had disappeared, he recognised the attraction for the dog.

In an open space amongst the bushes, sheltered from the breeze, there was a group of children and adults busily engaged in a picnic. They were already making a fuss of Scout and offering him a bit of sandwich. Baden marched cheerfully across to them and said, *"Don't feed him too much or he will not want his dinner."*

Baden was curious to know what the children were doing there. *"Is this a school picnic? Is this a reward because you've been a good class? Or are you taking a break from some natural history studies?"* The members of the picnic party exchanged apprehensive glances.

They were about to embark on a familiar dialogue. One of the children decided to respond.
"We are not from a school. We are from families who are educating their children as home."
"But you are all over five years of age so you have to attend school. That is the law, surely?"

One of the parents fielded this one. *"No, in fact the law says parents are required to arrange for the education of their children either at school or otherwise."*

Another member of the party joined in. *"It is education that is compulsory, not attending school."*
"Well, I can't think of anybody who has been educated that way."
"Well, there is the Queen, and we think that what is good enough for her is good enough for us."

Baden was a bit taken aback at the cheerful confidence of the children. But he wondered what they really knew.
"Right, in that case, answer me the following: what is the capital city of our country?"

The members of the party looked at each other. Should they tell the rude stranger to mind his own business, or to leave them alone, or to go and look it up for himself? On the other hand they were enjoying the company of Scout and if they wanted this to continue they would have to humour the stranger.

"I think we all know the answer - it is London."
"Fine, what is the name of the river that runs through London?"
"Well we went on that river in a tourist boat once, it is the Thames."
"Correct. Now, if I visit Edinburgh, which country am I in?"
One member answered good-humouredly, *"You would be visiting Scotland."*

Baden drew breath ready to pose another question. But before he could start, one of the children got in first and said, *"Is there anything else we can help you with?"* A gentle ripple of smiles ran round the party. Baden paused and reflected. Yes, he got the point. He was being a somewhat pompous ass.

One of the adults took pity on him.
"Have you got time to sit down and share a drink with us? Then we can tell you what home-based education is all about and you can tell us something about yourself."

"You are very kind," said Baden, remembering his manners.

"Scout is enjoying your hospitality, and I should like to follow his good example and accept your offer." They made room for him on a blanket and handed him a cup of tea.

"Have any of you've been to school at all?" he began. Yes, several of the party had been to school and then come out.
"How does your home education compare with the time you spent in school?"

Well, this was a much more intelligent question.
"First of all," said one member of the party, *"I find I get much more done. Often, I have learnt as much by coffee break at home, then in a whole day at school."*
"Or two days for that matter!" added someone else.
"School is a not an efficient place for learning because there are lots of unnecessary distractions and interruptions. A lot of time there is wasted time."

Another joined in. *"Another thing I have found is that I can continue my studies for long periods if I get involved in them, and not have to break my concentration just because a timetable says I must."*

"It is a much more learner-friendly situation," said one of the older children. *"I can take a break, when I need to, rather than when somebody else says so. And I don't have to put on special clothes – I think the right place for uniform is in the Army."*

"Talking of uniforms, I was in the Army for many years," said Baden. *"By the time I left I had risen to the rank of Lt. Col."*
Some of the children were quite curious and began to ask questions about his life in the Army.

But others wanted in know if they could take Scout for a walk. So Baden fitted the dog lead and gave into their care the scoop and the plastic bag in case they needed to clear up after Scout.

There now began a quite complicated double conversation with the children asking about life in the Army, and Baden asking about learning at home.

Baden wanted to know if their parents were teachers. He heard that in some cases this was true, and in other cases it was false. He also learned that the young learners became more and more proficient at managing their own learning, choosing from the wide range of learning resources and opportunities around in society.

He learned that they were not short of friends, and former school-friends used them to help out with their home-work as well as do other things together.

The adults explained that they did not try to replace a whole team of teachers themselves but found other people in the family or in the neighbourhood who were enthusiasts, or they just researched in the library or used the internet.
"But, because they become proficient at researching for themselves, I only need to 'teach' on a 'need to know basis," said one.

"What will you do about examinations?" said Baden.
"I can answer that," said one of the older children. *"I looked at correspondence courses and local college possibilities, but then I thought I ought to be able to plan my own courses. So, I got past examination papers and found the recommended textbooks and devised my own course of studies. Then I sat the exams at an External Candidates Centre."*
"How did you get on? asked Baden incredulously.
"Luckily, I got A grades in most of my subjects."

When Baden finally left the picnic, he thanked everyone for their hospitality. He felt he was a much wiser man than when he had set out for his walk earlier in the day. The children all seemed so mature, confident and well-informed.

Case-file eight

The public speaking contest

The day conference was drawing to a close. It had been a rich day with sessions on the latest research into home-based education, on the reasons for the rapid growth of this movement of the 'reluctant heretics', and the contrasts in methods of learning used by the families compared to the crowd instruction approach of schools.

The conference members, suitably refreshed after the afternoon tea break, drifted into the hall for the final session. At the front of the hall four young people were seated alongside each other at a table, waiting to begin the session. The conference organiser announced that this final session was to be a question and answer session involving the panel of four young people who had been educated at home. She invited the first question.

"How do young people who have been to school react to you being educated at home?"
Jasmin, who was 16, and had been educated at home for the last six years, began.
"It varies. Most of the young people I meet are at first curious and then envious. Some of my friends come around to our house for help with homework, not least because we have an excellent collection of reference and source books. Some of these are on loan from the library and others we have bought. A few of the people I meet are mildly abusive, saying I am either too snobbish to go to school, or alternatively too stupid to cope."

"How do you deal with the abusive ones?"
"Well, since it is often the same people who give out racial abuse, I deal with it in the same way. I either ignore it, or respond with some attempted disarming comment, quoting some of the facts to them."

The next question was,
"Do you feel you are ahead of those going to school?"
Roger, now seventeen, who had never been to school, decided to field this one.
"Generally, yes. When friends bring their homework to me for help, it seems like revision to me, and it doesn't present many problems. Next, they are often nervous with unfamiliar adults, so when we are out together, I find myself elected to deal with these situations."

"Do any of you do examinations or aim at going to university?" the next questioner wanted to know.
Ena was about to start university, so she responded to this one.
"I should be going to York University later this year. When I decided to try for university I enrolled at a local further education college for the examination subjects that I needed."

Andrew had something to say about this one.
"My plans are to study with the Open University. In some ways the Open University is the natural accompaniment to home-based education because the learning is itself home-based. It also means that I will not have to divert time and attention to obtaining GCSE examinations, or even 'A' levels, but move straight on from my own curriculum to the Open University curriculum which I can select from their catalogue. I am quite surprised that only a few home educated students follow this route."

The chairperson invited the next question. It came from the back of the hall.
"When some of you went to further education college, did you find it difficult to adjust?"
"Well," said Ena, *"the only problem I found was dealing with the other students' lack of enthusiasm for learning. My attitude in class was, here we have a teacher who has delved into the subject, so let us pick his or her brains with lots of questions. But my fellow students were alienated learners, and I think their curiosity and enthusiasm had been worn out by the formal instruction system a long time ago."*

"Do you think that you will educate your own children at home?"

"First of all," said Andrew, *"I'm not sure that I am up for being a father. The population of the world has doubled in the lifetime of my parents, and I am not sure about adding to the problem. But, supposing I did become a father, I think I would be looking to educate at home, provided my child agreed. This is because, in my experience, the school-based alternatives, whether state or private, are inferior substitutes. I have tried both, by the way. The few exceptions are hard to find."*

"There must be bad days at home," said one member of the audience, *"It can't be all sweetness and light!"*

"Yes, there are bad days at home," said Jasmin. *"There can be disagreements, disputes, and bad moods. But a bad day at home is a good deal better than a bad day at school. Actually better than most average days at school, come to think of it."*

The questions and answers went on for over an hour. Then the organiser took pity on the panel members, thanked them for a most interesting session, and closed the conference.

The panel members were taken for refreshments and a number of the adults joined them, both to congratulate them and to ask further the questions. One of the parents had a suggestion to offer.

"I was struck with your confidence as speakers. There is a forthcoming public speaking competition organised by the independent schools. And since the government keeps insisting that we are part of the independent sector if we choose to home educate, to get them off the hook of having to help us financially, I think we could enter a team of two for the competition. Is anyone interested?"

Eventually, two of the girls decided they were definitely interested. But they pointed out that they were not familiar with the style and rules of formal public speaking contests. They would need some help with this.

"Well, one local home-educating family is an actor family: both parents are professional actors, and I'm sure we can get some help from them. I will get the information and any entry forms, so that we can deal with the formalities."

The actors mentioned were only too pleased to help. They met with the girls to talk about the preparation they thought they needed.

And so the two girls were entered for the contest. They met with the actor family again in a local hall, and began to prepare for the public speaking contest. They picked up some useful tips about how to behave in a public speaking context, and enjoyed some helpful rehearsals.

Their confidence was boosted by the two actors praising their general confidence and fluency.
"Well," said Ena, *"we spend a lot of our time learning through conversation with each other, with our parents, and other people who come our way during each day."*

"I went to an independent school myself," said one of the actors. *"It was not an enjoyable or a positive experience, and that is one reason why we decided to educate our children at home. I think you have an excellent chance of doing well and even winning this contest."*

Apparently he was not the only one. A letter arrived from the organisers of the contest. It said that, on further consideration, they were not able to accept an entry from home-educated young people. It was felt that this was because they had unfair advantages!

Case-file nine

The inspection

The letter box rattled and a cascade of letters came through. Tony went over to the door and picked up the post from the mat. One of the letters looked rather official and it turned out to be a letter from the local education authority. It was suggesting a date when an inspector might call regarding their home-based education programme.

Previously, Tony had written to the local school explaining that the family would be taking over responsibility for the education of the children. This was the only action needed in England and Wales to signal the start of home-based education. Later they had received a letter from the education office acknowledging that the school had passed on the information and requesting some information about the proposed programme of studies.

The family members had taken a great deal of care in composing a letter explaining the approach to learning they proposed to adopt. They had joined the organisation *Education Otherwise*, and had found the advice about alternative approaches to home-based education, very helpful.

Tony remembered, vaguely, that an inspector might ask to visit, but he could not remember what had been said about it. So, he telephoned the *Education Otherwise* local co-ordinator, and asked for information and advice. The local co-ordinator explained that the local authority could not insist on a visit, but that most families decided that co-operation was probably the best policy, rather than risk the authorities starting to think they had something to hide.

Tony also learned that the meeting did not have to be at their home. It could be at the offices of the local education authority, or at some neutral venue, but that most families decided to invite an inspector to pay them a home visit. The inspectors, often found out to their surprise, however, that they had no right to demand a visit to the home.

Tony also gained the address and telephone number of somebody who had recently had a visit so that he could talk to them about their experience. He phoned the family concerned and they invited him and his family over. It was about half an hour's bus drive to reach the family, so the whole family went there the following afternoon.

They heard that the inspector had been very school-minded, expecting time-tables, textbooks, and regular periods of subject-based study. So the family had had to argue for their different point of view, and for the flexibility of their learner-managed approach. Tony was advised to 'learn his lines', and to be ready with arguments and evidence in case there was a difference of opinion. The family was advised to prepare carefully for the visit, and to have examples of work and learning resources to hand. Tony found out that the family they were visiting felt it should have prepared more carefully, and even had a rehearsal, to make sure they gave a convincing account of themselves.

Tony showed the letter and made a discovery. The name of the inspector who wanted to visit them was different. Because they lived in different parts of the city, they would not be getting the same inspector. Tony was not sure whether this was good news or bad news.

When the family got home, Tony telephoned the local co-ordinator again, who confirmed that different inspectors were responsible for different sectors of the city. But the inspector who would visit them was new, an unknown quantity. The co-ordinator volunteered to come around and conduct a rehearsal, and even to be there when the inspector visited, if that would be helpful. Tony and the members of the family felt comforted by this support.

They began to read around and prepare for the worst. They tried a few role-plays. Claire was a trained teacher, so she played the part of the inspector.

"Perhaps we can begin by looking at your timetable," she said.

"We do not work to a strict timetable," said Tony, *"we make a general plan for the week every Sunday evening, and then review it the following Sunday."*

"The approach of the authority, as laid down by the government, is that for learning to be effective it must be carefully structured," said Claire.

"We, too, accept the need for structure," said Tony, *"but we prefer emergent structures that develop by following the logic of the inquiry of the learner, rather than the artificially imposed structures of others. Our approach is more organic and eclectic."*

"But when you use books, or view instructional TV programmes, these have been structured by others," said Claire, in her best inspectorial voice.

"True," said one of the children, *"but we choose a particular book or programme because it fits our line of investigation, and reject those that don't."*

"Are there some lesson plans that I could see?" asked Claire.

"We do not work that way. We do not try to create 'school at home' by having formal instruction. Our approach is to get back to natural learning based on questions and enquiry. The adults rarely give any formal instruction except on a 'need to know basis' and then usually in response to a question that has been asked or a request for assistance," said Tony. *"We operate most of the time with a learner-managed learning, not a teacher-directed approach."*

"But that means there will large gaps in the knowledge of the children," protested the 'inspector' with mock horror.

"There are large gaps in the knowledge of everyone," replied Tony. *"But those who have regularly managed their own learning, will have become competent and confident researchers able to fill any gaps as and when it is necessary. Schooled children on the other hand become dependent learners who require others to organise the filling of gaps."*

Everyone found that they were quite enjoying the rehearsal and it continued over the evening meal. When the local co-ordinator visited them next day, she found that they gave quite a polished performance when she took on the role of the inspector.

The day of the visit arrived. At about 11 o'clock there was a knock on the door. The inspector had arrived. Tony opened the door, and invited Mrs Wilkinson to come in. Everyone was introduced, they all sat down and the proceedings began.

"I have recently joined the local authority as an inspector," said Mrs Wilkinson, *"and this is my first visit to a home-educating family. And I am really looking forward to it. I'm hoping to learn a lot from you, because my two children are not very happy at school, and seem to get unhappier by the day. It may not be long before my family joins the ranks of the home educators."*

"I think I will put the kettle on and make some coffee," said Tony. Obviously, this was not going to be the fierce interrogation that they had anticipated. It had all the makings of being an agreeable exchange of views.

Case-file ten

The home-education truant and the damage limitation programme

Every parent is a home-based educator until children reach the age of 5. After that, all parents are still home-based educators, although some are full-time, whereas others use schools for part of the time, during the weekdays, on those weeks the schools are open. For those who either choose to use schools, or necessity forces them to, do they need to consider a damage limitation policy?

I had to face this question when, some years ago now, my son reached the age of 5. His mother, Shirley, was an experienced infants teacher, and I was an experienced secondary teacher and teacher educator. With our insider knowledge, we both understood the serious limitations of compulsory mass schooling, whether state or private, and set out to offer our son a home-based education alternative. Ironically, he elected to try school, so his parents had to turn their attention to considering mounting a damage limitation programme.

Why was this necessary? A few years ago I wrote an article entitled "Schooling can seriously damage your education". I now think I was too cautious and should have entitled it, "Schooling **will** damage your education". The only question in my mind is how much damage will be done and in which dimensions.

There is **some** good news about schooling, however, as Everett Reimer indicated when he wrote, *"some true educational experiences are bound to occur in schools. They occur, however, despite school and not because of it."* Some teachers manage, despite our domination-riddled schooling system, to swim against the tide of restrictions and regulations, and create episodes of genuine humanity and genuine learning. I tried to be such a teacher and so did my wife Shirley. As my son put it, the good news was that he was able to *"find bits of treasure in the wreck"* of the schooling system, because of such teachers.

It is also true that the homes of some children are despotic or neglectful, so that even a coercive school provides a respite. Schools also provide a respite for parents from their children, so that they can pursue their careers, or whatever.

But the long-term effect of mass, compulsory coercive schooling is damage. As the New York prize-winning teacher, John Taylor Gatto put it in his book, *Dumbing Us Down: the hidden curriculum of compulsory schooling*, he was employed to teach bad habits. These ranged from bad intellectual habits, bad social habits, bad emotional habits, to bad moral and political habits. Neither the 'successful' pupils nor the 'unsuccessful' pupils escaped. For starters, he identified seven of these bad habits. I think they are worth repeating.

John Taylor Gatto recognised that what he was really paid to teach was an unwritten curriculum made up of seven ideas. The first was **confusion.** He was required to teach disconnected facts not understanding, infinite fragmentation not cohesion.

The second basic idea was **class position**. Children were to be taught to know their place by being forced into the rigged competition of schooling.

A third lesson was that of **indifference.** He saw he was paid to teach children not to care too much about anything. The lesson of bells is that no work is worth finishing: students never have a complete experience for it is all on the instalment plan.

The fourth lesson was that of **emotional dependency** for, by marks and grades, ticks and stars, smiles and frowns, he was required to teach children to surrender their wills to authority.

The next idea to be passed on was that of **intellectual dependency.** They must learn that good people wait for an expert to tell them what to do and believe.

The sixth idea is that of **provisional self-esteem**. Self-respect is determined by what others say about you in reports and grades; you are *told* what you are worth and self-evaluation is ignored.

The final, seventh lesson is that **you cannot hide**. You are watched constantly and privacy is frowned upon.

The consequence of teaching the seven lessons is a growing indifference to the adult world, to the future, to most things except the diversion of toys, computer games, 'getting stoned' as the height of having a good time, and violence. School, Gatto concludes, is a twelve-year jail sentence where bad habits are the only curriculum truly learned. School 'schools' very well but it hardly educates at all. Indeed, Paul Goodman entitled his book *Compulsory Mis-education*. But all this is good preparation for being gullible to the other controlling institutions, such as universities, but especially television, a theme developed in Gatto's book.

In contrast, home-based education can be seen as analogous to organic farming - a system with the toxins avoided. Our 'damage limitation', however, meant 'building up the immune system' to fight the toxins of the schooling system.

Other parents were puzzled as to why we saw what they regarded as 'good' schools, which today would no doubt get OFSTED approval, as 'educational impoverishment zones'. 'A good uniform means a good school', they declared. 'And probably a bad education based on uniformity', we responded. John Gatto had an explanation for this puzzled response: *"It is the great triumph of compulsory government monopoly mass-schooling that ... only a small number can imagine a different way to do things."*

So what did our policy of damage limitation look like? The first item was a principle: we would never pretend the school was right when it was wrong. If it proved necessary and with our son's approval, we would take the trouble to challenge the school when it was in the wrong, even if this meant we were labelled 'nuisance', 'interfering', or 'bad' parents. Part of this principle was never to shirk a dialogue with our son, about what was happening in school and its implications. Thus, when a teacher, unable to find a guilty party, punished the whole class, we pointed out that this was a common fascist procedure, but also why the authoritarian system pushed teachers into this corner.

The second item was a positive programme of activities to offset some of the bad habits John Gatto identified. To some extent, we just continued the programme of activities used between the ages of zero and five years, providing a learner-friendly environment that was personalised and democratic, stressing fun and happiness. This involved construction toys, board games, electronic games, watching TV programmes together, playing games in the garden or park - business as usual in fact.

We located out-of-school clubs and activities such as Judo groups, holiday soccer coaching courses, holiday table tennis events, and provided transport for groups of friends to go skating in the evening. One 'bit of treasure in the wreck' was the Local Education Authority's Saturday morning orchestra facility. This encouraged young musicians to gain experience with their own or with loaned instruments, in beginner ensembles and, eventually, leading to the senior orchestra. The LEA also had an Outdoor Centre in Wales and an Arts Residential Centre which were sources of worthwhile week-long courses.

The local naturalist society had regular Sunday outings to gardens, arboretums, bird-watching sites, ranging from woodland, to moorland, to seashore - even to sewage farms where we could view birds such as black terns - all in the company of enthusiasts. On occasion, we found ourselves at the Gibraltar Point Field Station for a weekend of investigation where father gained 'brownie points' for being the first to notice a rare red-backed shrike. The 'I Spy' booklets were a useful cheap resource but another favourite purchase was the magazine, *The Puzzler*.

We organised our own day trips to seaside, to parks with fun-fairs, to houses, to cities and museums, to sporting events ranging from the local soccer and cricket teams to the world table tennis championships. There were National Car Shows and the Birmingham Show to experience. We involved ourselves in a local amateur dramatic society that welcomed children to help out backstage. Also, the family, including grandparents, would often come along to meet the families, when I was researching home-based education. There were package holidays abroad to Sweden to visit friends, and also to Spain.

Perhaps none of this seems all that remarkable, and families across the social range do some selection of these things, according to their means and inclinations. But we consciously saw all these activities as opportunities for purposive conversation and mutual learning and an antidote to the effects of schooling. We could try to provide holistic and integrated learning to offset the fragmented approach of the school, and use any opportunities to practice the democratic skills of negotiation, consultation, accommodation, and co-operation - the skills that authoritarian schools usually discount and discourage.

What was achieved? Well, perhaps partial success could be claimed. Just choosing to be there, transformed the experience. At seven years, our son was telling us that, 'School did not get to him like the others, because he had an escape tunnel ready and waiting'. At eleven, he went to the Open Day at the secondary school where 300 children from the feeder schools in the district were in attendance, but he was conscious of being the only one making a decision whether to go or not. The others were conscripts. Later, we saw the head teacher, where my son informed him that he was giving the school a term's contract to see how things went. I came to realise that my son regarded the school in the same way that an anthropologist regards a tribe being studied - he was in the role of a participant observer.

The switch from school to further education college was eventually a considerable release from the domination of schooling, and independence of spirit and mind were better able to flourish. On the other hand, moving away to university meant that this institution just had a field day. The intellectual dependence Gatto talks about now asserted itself in the form of courses and modules requiring replication of approved material and rejecting any alternative or independent analysis as a threat to the authority of 'experts'. (During twenty years working in universities, this is what I observed happening as a matter of course, although pointing it out in committees was never well received.)

Is a damage limitation policy really necessary? And does every parent using schools, need one?   John Stuart Mill in *On Liberty* (1859, p177) observed that:

"A general State Education is a mere contrivance for moulding people to be exactly like one another, and as the mould in which it casts them is that which pleases the dominant power in the government, whether this be a monarchy, an aristocracy, or a majority of the existing generation ... it establishes a despotism over the mind, leading by a natural tendency to one over the body."

This seems to me to be just the opposite of an 'organic, toxin-free learning' outcome.

Case-file eleven

The researcher

The letter said,
"I have been reading some of your work, and I find we have a common interest in autonomous learning. Do you think we might meet up, and exchange ideas about this? I am trying to develop some psychologically-based research on the problem of trying to individualise learning."
And so a meeting was arranged.

When the initial pleasantries were over, the host and the researcher began to exchange experiences. They found common ground. Both had tried to establish autonomous learning systems in school settings and had found it very difficult. School is set up on the presumption of crowd instruction with learning managed by teachers. So any teacher who tried to develop individualised learning systems in classrooms, defied both the logic of the situation, and the credulity of colleagues.

What tends to happen is that the learners get at the most, a partial autonomy. Although the learners may become engaged on individually selected tasks, the study folders or assignments are actually devised by the teacher. The children are still being directed by the teacher, but in a more subtle way.

"The only time genuine autonomy happened," said the host, *"was when a learner asked if I had a study folder on a topic that particularly interested them, that did not seem to be present in the collection that I had available. At this point I would hand the learner a folder entitled, 'how to make your own study folder', and invite them to construct a new folder to add to the collection based on the missing topic."*

It was at this point the partial nature of the autonomy became apparent because the typical response of a learner was that they were not capable of planning their own study folder. Only when they had looked inside the 'how to make your own study folder' folder, did they begin to see how they might go about it.

"We would not need to try to individualise teaching in the classroom if other teaching methods were highly efficient," said the researcher.   *"But we know that the efficiency of formal instructional methods averages out at about 10 percent of the material being remembered, and that that it rarely exceeds 25 percent at the best of times, even with the most charismatic of teachers.   So the method has to be shored up with large quantities of homework and frequent and sustained revision."*

The host and the researcher agreed that even though individualised learning methods rarely occur in schools, the belief that somehow the learners should be working this way, will not go away. School policy statements still commonly refer to 'catering for the individual child'. Such statements sometimes wax eloquent about 'each learner has unique learning styles and learning problems, so that one of the teachers main tasks is to identify those characteristics and create appropriate learning conditions for each individual child'.   In the crowd control situation of the school, this proves to be more or less impossible.

"So, my research on autonomous learning is not getting very far," said the researcher. The host had a suggestion to make.
"There is one learning context where individualised learning is commonplace. I have been researching home-based education for a few years now, and there is a considerable amount of individual learner-managed learning to be seen. Families often start by trying to copy the formal instructional methods of the school, but then gradually learn that individual learner-managed learning is a happier and more effective way of going about things. Some parents end up saying that they only give any formal instruction on a 'need to know' basis, or in answer to a learner's question."

The researcher was interested and wanted to know how he could begin to look into this phenomenon. Well, as luck would have it, the host had received a letter from a home-educating family offering to put up for a week, a student who wanted to study them for a project. The family thought it would be an interesting and mutual learning experience. The researcher took the letter and agreed to make contact. This somewhat chance encounter opened up new avenues of research into autonomous learning that led to variety of several research papers and a book.

One important finding was the role of 'purposive conversation' in autonomous learning. After his time with the first family, the researcher wrote:

"What impressed me most during that week was that nothing much seemed to happen, on the surface at least, especially when compared with the sense of purposeful industry you get when you look into a typical classroom. There was no timetable or sequentially designed programme of learning activities within a planned curriculum. We went for walks. The two children, aged 11 and 13, certainly read a lot. They spent some time working on their own projects. There were various outside activities, including band practice. One of them was doing a project on infant development and was helping a neighbour with her newborn baby. There were friends around after school and there was a schools musical Eisteddfod which one of them took part in ... What struck me most of all during the week was the constant opportunity for informal learning, especially through social, often incidental conversation... One day, for example, we were all sitting around the kitchen table engaged in our separate activities. Topics of conversation, as often as not unrelated to what we would be doing, kept cropping up. Among other things, we discussed slavery, Nelson Mandela, salt-water crocodiles and levels of ground water... and whether to go down to the shop for some doughnuts."

The research on learning systems shows that discussion is an effective method of learning with over a 50 percent efficiency level. This 'purposive conversation' amongst adults and children that the researcher encountered, is rare in schools. Indeed, for a considerable amount of time, conversation is forbidden so that the learners can listen to the teacher's expositions. But in the first few years of life, children learn a tremendous amount without being deliberately taught, much through social, informal everyday conversation. Although we do not deliberately teach children their mother tongue, they still learn its highly complex structure.

When the host and the researcher met again a few years later they reviewed what they had learnt in the meantime.

"I have noted over ten reasons why home-based education is so successful," said the host.   *"Your research has confirmed the important gain in the methodology adopted in families. Even in the cases where the approach remains formal, using ready-made courses, there is still the gain of plenty of purposive conversation."*

The researcher agreed.   He then made a further significant point.
"There is an interesting link with the various studies of high achievement and the development of people who become identified as 'genius', and the approach of home-based educators. To some extent, the regime often found in home-based education has characteristics reminiscent of those found by the Smithsonian research into the learning regimes of the genius.

"H.G.McCurdy of the University of North Carolina identified three key factors.   The first was, a high degree of individual attention given by parents and other adults and expressed in a variety of educational activities, accompanied by abundant affection.   Secondly, only limited contact with other children outside the family but plenty of contact with supportive adults. Thirdly, there was an environment rich in, and supportive of, imagination and fantasy.   In all this, purposive converstion played a key role."

The host agreed.   *"McCurdy concluded that the mass education system of the USA based on formal methods and inflexible organisation, constituted a vast experiment in reducing all these three factors to the minimum.   The result was the suppression of high achievement.   Home-based education seemed to be busily reinstating the three factors.*

"In the end, the 'amateur' home-educating parents are outperforming the 'professional' teachers, because the latter are asked to try and educate in a context which guarantees limited results."

Case file twelve

The head teacher

Basil had really chosen the module entitled *Alternative Educational Systems*, as a bit of light relief from the heavy nature of the rest of his course for the Masters Degree in Education. But so far, it had proved to be more interesting than all the other modules put together.

This last session on 'the pupils' perspective on teaching and schooling' had given him an idea for the essay he would have to submit at the end of the module. He wondered what would happen if he, as the head teacher, engaged in a consultation exercise with some of the pupils in his school.

He hung back at the end of the session to talk to the tutor. Yes, the tutor thought it was an excellent idea, and lent him a copy of the book, *The School That I'd Like*, edited by Edward Blishen.

A week or two later he had completed the assignment. He had found it very revealing to talk to the pupils in his school about what it was like to be on the receiving end. As a result of the consultation he had in mind to suggest a few modifications at next week's staff meeting. He would spare them from having to read his assignment on the issue for homework.

He handed in his assignment, and settled down for the evening session. It was entitled 'The growing phenomenon of home-based education'. Well, it was certainly an interesting topic, but he doubted if it would have any relevance to him personally, as the head teacher of a secondary school.

But soon he had entered a whole new fascinating world. It was a world where children could develop their particular interests and strengths, manage their own learning, use quite different methods of learning, such as purposive conversation, and make maximum use of their own personal learning styles. They could use the community as their resource, access our now information-rich society at will, and use the world of knowledge as a catalogue curriculum. It was heady stuff.

When he got home, his wife and two young daughters greeted him with questions about what 'wild' ideas had he been exposed to this time. So he told them all the things he could remember about home-based education. He got out his notes to confirm some of the ideas.

They were all very intrigued and then began to speculate about what would happen if they began to educate at home. The youngest daughter, aged 6, said,
"I would be able to spend more time on my music. That would make me much happier."
"Do you feel unhappy at school?" asked mother.
"Well, not really unhappy, but I do feel a bit deadened by it all."
"When the tutor was talking about the pupils' view of school, the other week, he said that for some of the pupils all the time, and for all of the pupils some of the time, the classroom seems like cage from which there is no escape. Is that something to do with it?"

The other daughter, aged 7, joined in.
"When you're doing things in school that don't make much sense or are not very interesting, or you know already, it does seem like a cage."
"How often is that?" asked mother.
"Well, most of the time, really."

The younger daughter had something more to say.
"Before I went to school, we learnt so much at home doing things together. I don't think I learn so much now. There's so much time spent just ... waiting. You wait for the teacher to come, you wait for things to be handed round, you wait to be asked to answer the teacher's question, you wait around in the playground ... "

Later on, after the girls had gone to bed, Basil and Cara talked some more. They had both felt that some of the life and sparkle had been going from their daughters in the last few months.

Now, in talking with the girls, they began to see reasons why. Moreover, in talking about what learning at home might be like, some of the life and sparkle, that they had noticed had gone from their daughters, had started to return to the girls. Cara was a music teacher but declared that this idea might be important enough for her to give up her post for the time being, to be the anchor person at home. They could manage on one salary for a few years.

Basil arrived at the university. Tonight's session was entitled, 'Democracy and power sharing in schools'. He settled down to hear how schools in other countries, such as Denmark, had not only class councils, schools councils, but student unions, National Federations of students, and, in general, a high-level of participation in the decision-making of the school by the learners. By the end of the session his mind was now spinning with a new idea. He stayed on to talk to the tutor.

"Supposing I set about trying to make my school more democratic, with this be a suitable subject for study?" he wanted to know.

"It would be quite a unique study," said the tutor, *"and if it is well done, it would give you a PhD and probably a book too. I do not know of any case studies of this kind."*

"By the way," said Basil, *"I have some surprising news - at least it's a big surprise to me. I shall be joining the ranks of the home-based educators. We discussed it as a family and looked into it further. We made contact with some local families and went to see them.*

"Cara decided this was so important, that she would be prepared to give up her job as a music teacher, because the more we discussed the idea, the more the life and sparkle began to come back into their daughters."

"How will you explain this to your board of governors?" asked the tutor.

"I shall blame you," said Basil, *"and wax eloquent about the need for a more flexible, learner-responsive, and family-friendly learning system!*

"We shall not be turning our backs of the idea of schools, so

much as moving forward to a system that encourages episodes of home-based education, flexi-time, more invitational and more democratic schools ... how well have I learnt the lines? "

"I think you have learnt them pretty well," said the tutor.   *"You could start with some sound bites such as, the next learning system means, 'anybody, any age, any time, any place, any pathway, any pace.'"*
"I think I had better just write all that down," said Basil, *"it might come in very useful."*

Case file thirteen

The T.V. show

"Welcome to this edition of the Angela and Jonathan show. Today, we shall be looking into the idea of educating children at home," said presenter Angela.

Presenter Jonathan continued, *"We have in the studio a number of families who have taken the decision to educate their children at home instead of sending them to school, as well as a researcher and some members of the public.*

"Some viewers may be surprised to find that school is not compulsory. The law in our country states that education is compulsory, either by attendance at school, or otherwise. The government is rather dishonest in not making this plain to everyone. In an expensive exercise, sending a booklet to all parents about education, it failed to mention the home-education option at all."

"The organisation Education Otherwise is a self-help group for those who choose education at home," explained Angela, as she walked over towards one of the people in the audience. *"Hazel is a member of the council of Education Otherwise. 'Hazel, what kinds of people decide to educate at home?'"*

"Many people suppose that it will be middle-class families with a good income level," replied Hazel. *"But, in fact we find that people from all walks of life are home-educating. And the average income of the families is below the national average, not least because one parent usually needs to be at home, rather than earning."*

"Some people would see that is quite a sacrifice - reducing the family income," observed Angela.

Hazel explained, *"One person's 'sacrifice' is another person's 'investment'.   Many parents say they are investing in their children's happiness and growth as independent, confident people."*

Jonathan took over.   *"Kevin, how long have you been educated at home?"*
"I last went to school when I was seven, that was three years ago."
"What did you dislike about school?"
"It was not right for me.   There was never enough time to finish tasks.   And we wasted a lot of time just waiting for things to happen.   I get more done by coffee break at home, then in a whole day at school."
"Don't you miss your friends?"
"No, I have plenty of friends.   Some of those from school still call around, and we do things together."

The camera shot switched to Angela.   *"Melanie, why did your children come out of school?"*
"I became more and more desperate as I saw the school was not working for Brian and Sally.   They were losing confidence in themselves.   There were bits of bullying that the school seemed quite uninterested in sorting out.   Then I saw a magazine article about a family who were very happy with their home-based education.   So we talked it over as a family for several weeks and then decided we must take the plunge."
"How did it work out?"
"We seem to take to it like ducks to water.   We have no regrets."

The man sitting next to Melanie wanted to join in.   *"I am alarmed at all of this.   School is there to socialise people, to toughen them up for the real world, not to make people happy. It is there to make them learn what society needs them to learn."*
"You sound just like Bernhard Rust!" said Melanie.
"Who is he?"
"He was the education minister for the Third Reich."
"I think that is offensive."
"No more offensive than telling us that the world is nasty, tough and grim and that we should fatalisically put up with it and train our children to put up with it.   I hope our home-educated children will work for a better world rather than be the sad kind of conformists who just perpetuate the present one.

The producer switched to presenter Jonathan, who said, *"Pauline, you have been doing some research into families that educate at home. How well do they do?"*

"Well, there is good news, and then there is good news. On the kinds of tests that schools use, children who are being educated at home for two years or more, will be, on average, two years ahead of their schooled counterparts. They may be as much as ten years ahead, especially when the family concentrates entirely on school-type academic studies. Then, in addition, the children gain bonus skills, such as conversational competence, imagination, creativity, independence, emotional maturity, more sophisticated social skills, and positive self-image."

"None of this puts our schools and teachers in a very favourable light," observed Jonathan.
"My research has led me to the view that schools are now out-of-date, and the teachers are in the role of victims who are asked to make an obsolete system work."

Angela came back on screen, talking to another parent. *"Alfie, do you see schools as obsolete?"*
"I cannot think of any other situation than school where you are forced to spend time with people of one age for hours on end," said Alfie. *"Then, you are forced to learn things because other people say so, irrespective of whether it will actually be any use to you. At home, my children direct their own learning, and develop skills as researchers delving into any knowledge they have need for."*

Angela turned to Alfie's daughter. *"Alice, do you miss school?"*
"Well, I've never actually been. When I was five, we all talked about the possibility of going to school, but I was so happy learning at home, we decided not to. I talked to other children at school, and visited a few schools, and it all seemed very restrictive. Whilst the other children are stuck in classrooms, we are out and about in the libraries, museums, parks and other places, learning freely."

"What have you learnt out and about in society, that you would not have learnt at school?"
"Well, there is sailing. When we were walking around a lake

one day, we watched a young woman sail to the jetty and tie-up her dinghy. I began to talk to her, and to explain that I had always been interested in sailing, but had not yet had the opportunity to start. So she took us out on the lake and I went on to join the sailing club as a junior."

Jonathan appeared on screen again. *"We are going to have to call an end to this fascinating discussion, as time has run out - it's a bit like school here, the timetable and the clock are our gods.*

"But I have been thinking about my own two children, who do not find that school does all that much for them. So if some of the families are not in too much of a hurry to leave, I think I'd like to talk to you some more ..."

Case file fourteen

The examination

One of the favourite activities of Lennie, when the Kingston family went to town, was browsing in the local W.H.Smith shop. They would look at the video section, the CD section and the books department. The last time he went he got very interested in a book on geography. It was his 14th birthday soon. If he got some money for presents, he decided he would buy the book.

Well, he did get enough money and he spent some of it on the book. He spent the next two days studying the book and trying out some of the exercises. He took the results of his labours to his parents to see what they had to say. His father, Lance pointed out that the book was part of a GCSE 'O' level course, and told Lennie he thought he was doing very well with the exercises.

"You could go on and do this course and sit the examination at the end. We could write to the examination board for some past examination papers, for the subject report, and for the standards booklet which would give examples of answers to exam questions which were awarded different grades. These help you work out just what examiners are looking for."

Lance was not a teacher, but he had been reading the newsletters from *Education Otherwise* and the *Home Education Advisory Service.* He had remembered some of the details from an article on studying for exams at home. Lennie agreed that it was worth looking into.

When all the materials arrived from the examination board, the whole family had a good look at the examination papers. Then they looked at the syllabus and the other items, including the notes of guidance.

"We could find a correspondence course, or we could inquire at the local further education college, or find a tutor, or find an internet-based course," said Lance.

"Do we need to?" asked Lennie. *"We are all used to organising our own learning, so I think I could organise an examination course. If I count up the number of weeks to the exam, and allow a few weeks for revision, I can allocate the topics on the syllabus for each of the weeks."*

Lennie had already noticed that he could do quite a few of the questions already. He checked some of the exercises he had done against the examples of answers to exam questions provided by the examination board. His results came out rather well, and is made him confident that he could cope. He knew that he would get any help, support and encouragement that he needed from his parents.

Lennie entered himself for the examination at the Cambridge Open Centre in ten month's time. He was surprised to find that the local further education college did not accept private candidates. Private candidates have to pay entry fees which are quite high, but the family thought it was worthwhile to see how Lennie got on.

The work was pretty interesting. His parents followed some of the course with him and jokingly suggested that perhaps they should register for the examination, too. They found some useful supporting material and ideas on some Internet sites.

On the day of the examination, the family decided to make an outing of the visit to Cambridge. The Cambridge Open Centre was in the library of Lady Margaret House, which the examination board had borrowed for the purpose. There were several other home-educated candidates who had come for the examination as well as a few older 'mature' students.

When they all met up afterwards, Lennie was smiling. *"I was surprised how many of the questions I had already answered in doing the exercises. And I thought I knew the answers to the others. I think I might have done reasonably well."*

All the members of the family were very pleased on his behalf. Lance wanted to know what Lennie would like to do as a celebration. *"When we get home,"* said Lennie, *"can we have an Indian take-away?"* Everybody agreed that was an excellent idea.

Eventually the results came through. Lennie's confidence was justified. He had gained an A grade. Next year, he decided, he was now ready to take a group of five or six subjects.

Case file fifteen

The Esperanto connection

A small number of home-educating families include Esperanto as part of their learning programme. They do this for two reasons. Firstly it enables them to correspond with some families all over the world. Such families tend to have the same value system, being devoted to international understanding and co-operation.

Secondly, the research shows that a knowledge of Esperanto enables you to learn other European languages, such as French Italian and Spanish, at will, and in half the time it would take otherwise.

The Dobbins family had decided to educate the two younger members at home on the advice of the two elder children who had been through school. They declared that it must be possible to have a better education than the one they had experienced. They offered to help out with any attempts at home-based education.

The parents had a long association with Esperanto and the children had caught their enthusiasm. Because they were educating at home, they were not restricted by the requirements of any National Curriculum. They could add Esperanto to their studies without any fuss. The mother helped the children work through the beginners course and the family also played Esperanto games together.

The Esperanto newsletter arrived in the post. Some bits were in English and other parts were in Esperanto. By now, the children could make sense of most of the parts of the newsletter written in Esperanto. The parents had suggested that they were now ready to correspond with people in other countries. The newsletter seemed to contain an ideal match. A family in Poland with children of the same age as the Dobbins family, were advertising for pen pals.

So, today's activity in Esperanto would be composing letters of introduction. Everybody set to work with great enthusiasm. Then they compared their letters with each other. They read them out in turn and made notes of any suggestions, comments or corrections. Next, they raided the family photograph collection to find some that they could send with the letters.

The family in Poland were quick to respond, so within a few days they all had replies and photographs too. The letter to mother contained an invitation, which was repeated in all the other letters, to come to Poland and to visit them in Gdansk. Then they could all practice their Esperanto face-to-face. Everyone thought that this was a splendid idea, so in their letters of reply they all accepted.

The planning for the visit to Poland began in earnest. They found that they could travel by coach, by rail or by plane. It was also possible to combine travel by plane to Berlin and then on by train. But they decided that they could afford to go by plane direct to Gdansk.

Father, with some help from the family members, had designed and marketed a wood-based construction kit. Although it could be used as a toy, it had a more serious purpose as a technical design aid. To some extent, it was a wooden version of the Meccano metal construction kits. So they decided to take one along as a present to the Polish family.

As their plane approached Gdansk, they appeared to be landing in a field and approaching a large shed. Gdansk was quite a small airport. After they had passed through customs they saw the Polish family holding a card with the name Dobbins on it. They were made to feel very welcome and they were surprised how well they could communicate with each other using their Esperanto. Nevertheless, they were all glad that they had come equipped with their Esperanto dictionaries.

The Polish family was very interested in the home-based education programme of the Dobbins family. They explained that this was only recently possible in Poland since the Russians had left.   Until then they were subject to a rigid national curriculum, endless formal teaching, aggressive inspections, and endless testing.

The Russian regime, like the Nazi regime before it, had made home-based education a criminal offence and had also abolished small schools.   To obtain conformity, they insisted on large schools.   But now these totalitarian ideas were giving way to something more flexible, and small schools were making a comeback.

But the Polish family was surprised to hear that the UK schooling system had been adopting an approach very similar to the Russian system.   They were taken aback and wanted to know why there were no democratic schools in UK, instead of the totalitarian-style domination-riddled ones.   Of course, they were told, this was part of the reason for the Dobbins family adopting home-based education – to get away from the rules, routines and regimentation approach.

Later, they presented the Polish family with the construction kit. It was well received.   The father, Tomasz, showed a particular interest because he was involved in the wood industry.   He declared that he would be able to send wood to England for the kits at a better price than the one they were currently charged. Also, he was quite sure that they could sell some kits in Poland and so become the local agents.

And so the Esperanto connection eventually gave birth to … a trading partnership.

Appendix

Crown Court Simulation on Education

Written by Mary Dalton, Allen Edge, Cathy Jockel, Roland Meighan and Rodney Seville

Origin of this role-play

This role-play is designed for secondary pupils aged fourteen to eighteen and can be used either as a general introduction to the British Legal System, or as a basis *for* examining basic attitudes towards education. Role-plays help pupils to explore issues. This role-play poses several vital questions for practitioners and consumers of present-day state controlled education - whether or not there are viable alternatives to formally structured and institutionalised education. If there are, which alternatives are the most valid, and finally are the various alternatives valid in different circumstances and with different people? This simulation might serve as an introduction to, or as part of, a course on the sociology of education.

This role-play was inspired by a court case heard at Worcester Crown Court in 1981 involving the issues outlined here. Although the actual case heard in court involved a family similar to the one portrayed, this role-play is not a verbatim account of the case. Simplification has been necessary to make the issues and personalities accessible to secondary school pupils.

Preparation for: *"Newtown Crown Court;*
Hilary and Michael Harvey v. The Crown"

For class work all of the pupils would need to be aware of the information outlined below, under 'Background to the case'. *This is probably best achieved through the distribution of a worksheet containing the information the day before* 'the hearing.' *At this stage, role-cards could also be distributed to pupils chosen to act out the various roles. The aim is to start the role-play as quickly as possible from* 'cold.' *The roles outlined are:*
1) Judge John Smyth Q.C.
2) Lord Peter Redman - Defence Counsel
3) Mrs. Hilary Harvey

4) Mr. Mike Harvey
5) Marian Harvey
6) Dr. Donald Hanimeg
7) Dr. Agatha Hobbes
8) Mr. Paul Neal - Prosecuting Counsel
9) Mr. Reginald Jones
10) Mr. Charles Henry

We would recommend that to increase the significance of the role-play activity that the pupils be taken on a visit to a Crown Court. This will provide an experience of 'court atmosphere' and some impression of the varying importance of certain principal people in the court. A plan of the court at Worcester has been included to assist with the seating arrangements of pupils during the role-play. Depending on class size some teachers may like to have fewer pupils sitting in the 'public gallery' and instead expand the number of pupils directly involved in the simulation. This involves the writing of new role-cards with two possibilities suggesting themselves immediately, both of them expanding the quality and character of the follow-up work with a class:

1) **Justices of the Peace**
Two J.P.s could be introduced into the court creating the possibility of a split vote, which is a principal ground for appeal. The introduction of J.P.s could also lead to an analysis of the role and position of J.P.s within the legal system, the perceived problems and advantages of non-expert interpretation of legal problems, and finally the grounds of appeal against judgements.

2) **The Press**
A number of pupils can be given role-cards delegating them to write a report of the hearing in a certain style. A preliminary study of the various styles of reporting commonly used in the major dailies, would be useful. Analysis of the reports produced can follow and lead to an analysis of press bias and its implications, freedom of the press, and why some cases are heard 'in camera'.

Background to the case

1. The Harvey Family's Appeal
The Harveys are appealing against a conviction to comply with a school attendance order. This appeal is the latest in a series of hearings dating back several years. The Harveys are educating their four children at home, because their experience of normal schooling was found to be too stressful, in accordance with the principles of the autonomous approach to education - a direct challenge and alternative to the traditional and formal methods of the state education system.

2. The Autonomous Approach to Education

Advocates of the autonomous approach to education hold that worthwhile education can be self-directed in a stimulating, unstructured but caring environment. Learning occurs in response to the difficulties of problem-solving. The child's curiosity is the key to its development - curiosity about the world generating the need to understand and acquire skills to pursue experimentation and inquiry into the surrounding environment. The skills required by the children themselves and by society are thus learnt as and when they are required, rather than in some imposed artificial order.

3. Family Background

Mr. and Mrs. Harvey have tried to create a home environment, in the country to the west of Newtown, where free inquiry by the children is possible. Their life is therefore their education. The children's home is an attractive farmhouse with extensive outbuildings and a two acre smallholding. The children are responsible with their parents for the development of this site and this development is a source of interest and experiment that the Harveys believe is necessary to make 'the autonomous education approach' work.

4. Family History

From the beginning of their school education, in varying degrees, the children reacted against the school. They felt violated, threatened, and in danger of losing their individuality. Emotional problems in the children, and family tensions, developed. Eventually, Mr. and Mrs. Harvey felt that they and their children were no longer able to cope with the pressures exerted on the children from state schools, but not until Marian, the eldest child, had been threatened with placement in a school for emotionally disturbed children. Since then, in spite of several court actions, the Harveys have refused to allow the Local Education Authority (L.E.A.) to test the educational attainment of their children, as the children find this kind of experience threatening and unnerving. The Harveys are therefore now following a system of autonomous education to educate their children.

5. The Harveys and the Law

The Harveys appeal against the conviction for failing to send their children to school is based not only on their belief that their approach to education is a genuine alternative to that offered by the state system, but also because they believe that they comply with the requirements of the 1944 Education Act. This Act requires that pupils must receive full-time education at school, *or otherwise,* according to age, aptitude and ability. The Harveys believe that the education that their children have undergone has equipped them well for life according to their ages, aptitudes and abilities, and furthermore has given them a flexible and original approach to problem solving that is increasingly required by a fast changing and increasingly complex society, and less and less provided by standard education. The Harveys also point out that The European Convention on Human Rights (Article 2 Protocol 1) states:

'No person shall be denied the right to education. In the exercise of any function which it assumes in relation to education and teaching the state shall respect the right of parents to ensure such education and teaching in conformity with their own religious and philosophical convictions'.

The Harveys hope that if their appeal is successful, and the court concludes that they are providing an adequate education for their children and can continue to do so, that the case will be used as support for other families wishing to educate their children at home.

Crown Court Simulation Plan of Court

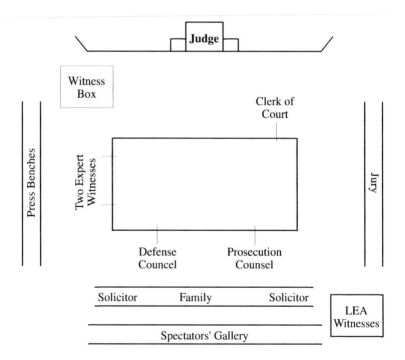

The above is a direct plan of the court room at Worcester Crown Court. It will provide a useful guide in the arrangement of a classroom when this role-play is used. We recommend that the teacher take on the role of the Clerk of the Court in order to supervise proceedings while remaining as unobtrusive as possible.

Role-plays

The names used below are fictitious, but are based on characters present at Worcester Crown Court at the time of the case.

Judge John Smyth Q.C.

Judge John Smyth Q.C. is fifty-eight. He was educated at Charterhouse public school and Clare College, Cambridge. He runs a workman-like court and will not tolerate sloppiness in procedure or analysis of the statutes. Judge Smyth does have a sense of humour, however, although he remains a stickler for formality. He established a routine of hard work early in life and is one of the most copious and accurate taker of notes amongst judges on the circuit, and is also well known for his penetrating and astute questioning of both defendants and witnesses as well as counsel.

Judge Smyth's education enabled him to indulge in much private study, although formal education was still very much a part of his learning. He can, therefore, be said to have a fairly open mind on the subject of autonomous education. He recognises that formal schooling can be a traumatic experience as he had a 'rough time', as he describes it, at Charterhouse.

Judge Smyth is aware that in his judgement of this case he may well be setting a precedent for many more families in the country who wish to educate their children at home. Consequently he is going to treat the case very seriously.

The Harvey Family: Hilary Harvey

Mrs. Harvey is 38. She had some success at school, learning quickly, and finally leaving with seven 'O' Levels and one 'A' Level. She worked as a photographer with a local newspaper, but left the job after having her first child. Also, as she and her husband realised school was not suitable to their children, she felt that this was a reason to stay at home to help educate them. She now works in the house and on the smallholding. She is very active in local environmental groups such as *The Friends of the Earth* and the anti-nuclear movement. Hilary gets on very well with all her family - they are all on an equal footing with each other, which works very well. She believes that the approach the family has adopted to education has suited the needs of each child and has allowed them to develop as individuals with skills, which are very relevant to today's society.

Mike Harvey

Mr. Harvey is also 38. He did not enjoy his schooldays, having difficulty in learning to read and write and was consequently placed in a remedial class throughout his time at school. He is now literate. He learnt plumbing skills from his father and is now a self-employed plumber. He earns enough money for the family to live on fairly easily and so is able to spend a lot of time on the smallholding with them helping the children when his assistance is needed. Neither Mike nor Hilary have any reservations about autonomous education for their children or for any others.

Marian Harvey

Marian is the eldest of the Harvey children. She is now sixteen and so able to appear in court to give evidence. Also, of course, she is no longer the subject of a school attendance order, no longer being of compulsory school age. Marian attended primary school for about three months but did not enjoy it, feeling that in the school nobody was really concerned about her as an individual. She became very withdrawn and as a result had difficulties in reading and writing. Because of this she was placed in the school's remedial department and then threatened with placement in a special school for emotionally disturbed children. Because her parents realised that her withdrawal was a result of school experience they knew that this would not help her at all. Marian was kept at home from then on.

When the local authority later decided to take Marian and the other children into care, the family moved to a smallholding in another L.E.A. area. This authority, however, put a School Attendance Order on all of the children and over the last six years the family have been fighting the authority through the courts.

Marian is giving evidence for herself and on behalf of her brothers and sister: Mark, aged fifteen, Patricia, aged thirteen and Simon, aged ten. She herself is an expert baker, plumber, typist and clarinetist. She has also run a sideline rearing hens, and can repair and maintain cars amongst other things. She has many good friends in the locality, and plays in the orchestra of a nearby town. She does not believe that she has suffered socially or in any other way from autonomous education.

The Prosecuting Counsel and Witnesses

Mr. Paul Neal

Mr. Neal is the prosecuting counsel. He is a young, hardworking barrister, eager to prove himself in this case, but he realises he has a difficult job for he is up against a barrister with many more years experience. Nevertheless he believes he has a strong case, it being based on a previous conviction of the Harveys in the magistrates court for failing to comply with a school attendance order. Some of the main points Mr. Neal and the prosecuting witnesses will be trying to establish are:
1) The children are lacking in the essential skills of reading and writing.
2) That the children's education is not systematic.
3) Are the children different from those receiving state education?

4) If the children are unable to cope with stressful situations in school, how will they manage to cope in adult life when they are likely to meet even greater strains?

Mr. Reginald Jones

Mr. Jones is an educational psychologist and has worked for a number of years with the L.E.A. Prior to this he was employed as a teacher. He enjoys his work, but does not have sufficient time to keep up-to-date with new educational theories. During the course of his work he did meet and assess the Harvey children once, and consequently recommended that they be sent to a special school, which he felt would best suit the children's needs. Mr. Jones believes that if the children do have learning difficulties a special school would be more suited to tackle their problems than home education. He also believes that the children's education is haphazard and unsystematic, and although he admits they do have skills, he still feels they are not receiving an adequate education.

Mr. Charles Henry

Mr. Henry has worked for the L.E.A. for nearly twenty years. He fully appreciates what the Harveys are trying to achieve, but strongly maintains that the L.E.A. feels the parents are not providing their children with an adequate education. Mr. Henry believes that assessment of the children must take place to enable the L.E.A. to ascertain if they are being educated sufficiently. He is also sceptical that anybody who cannot read and write to a certain level can be said to be adequately educated.

The Defence Counsel and Witnessess

Lord Peter Redman

Lord Redman is counsel for the defence. He makes no secret that his sympathies lie with the family, and has consequently taken a keen and lively interest in their case. Lord Redman is a barrister of long standing and is very experienced in court procedure and skilful in his questioning of witnesses and the presentation of his case. Some of the main points that Lord Redman and the defence witnesses will be trying to establish are:

1) School is outdated in its education of children, being no longer able to meet the needs of the children or of present day society.

2) Education at home can work in many cases, especially for children who do not find the present school system satisfactory.

3) Education at home can provide young people with skills which are directly relevant to everyday needs.

4) Learning through everyday experiences encourages interest in learning and eradicates boredom which many children experience from learning about things they may not be interested in.

Dr. Donald Hanimeg

Dr. Hanimeg is a university lecturer of many years standing. He lectures in sociology of education and is also responsible for the training of teachers on postgraduate courses. He is the author of many books on sociology and education, and is highly regarded as an educationalist. He became involved with the Harvey family as a member of 'Alternative Education' - a group set up in 1976 to assist families who educate their children at home. He has become a personal friend of the family and has been involved in their fight with the authorities for several years. Dr. Hanimeg strongly believes that education at home is a viable means of educating young people, and provides a very adequate alternative to standard school education in providing young people with a variety of essential skills and experiences.

Dr. Agatha Hobbes

Dr. Hobbes was a teacher for many years, but left the profession because she became increasingly disillusioned with the educational process. Dr. Hobbes has since become involved in educational research and is the author of several well known and widely read books on the education system. In her books Dr. Hobbes argues that secondary schools are now seriously out of step with the needs and aspirations of modern youth. She objects to the predominance of academics in education, and the system of measuring and assessing a single aspect of personal ability through such means as examinations. She also argues that failure to succeed in examinations and tests can have a damaging affect on young people, as they will immediately he labelled as failures.

(This simulation was first published as an article in Social Science Teacher in 1983.)

Further reading from Educational Heretics Press

Those Unschooled Minds:
home-educated children grow up

by Julie Webb

The book is based on interviews with 20 home-educated people. They are now in their twenties or thirties except for one, a man who older. Julie Webb first spoke to about a quarter of them as teenagers in the early 1980s. She wanted to find out what sort of lives they were leading now, and hear their reflections on the process of home educating - and whether they would consider home educating their own children.

The people who are the subject of Julie's book, home-educated for part or all of their years of compulsory education, come from families with many different reasons for ditching the orthodox structure. The common factor in their approach is the intention of replacing the *"one size fits all"* philosophy, with learning that emerges from the abilities and interests of the individual, deepening and expanding as the child matures.

ISBN   1-900219-15-8   £9-95

Doing It Their Way:
home-based education and autonomous learning

by Jan Fortune-Wood

Autonomous education allows children and young people to develop the lifelong habit of being self-directed and intrinsically motivated learners. This is a process that looks remarkably unlike anything we expect to see from our schools. Yet it has a long tradition in the fields of education, philosophy and psychology. The core to understanding autonomous education is, I contend, the primacy of intrinsic motivation. In addition, it demands a broad definition of education and an environment of non-coercion.

The wider questions of the effect of autonomous home education on lifestyle are introduced, focussing on eradicating the lines of demarcation between education and life and looking at practical issues such as common limits on autonomy, the use of television and computers, and the role of play.

Rev. Dr. Jan Fortune-Wood currently works as a parish priest in an outer estate parish in Birmingham.

ISBN   1-900219-16-6   £11-95

The Next Learning System:
and why home-schoolers are trailblazers

by Roland Meighan

"I started reading it at 10 o'clock at night and I could not put it down until I had finished it, so you cost me some sleep ..."
Colin Rose, Director, Accelerated Learning Systems

"Any one who takes a look at our educational system knows that it must change profoundly. We need fundamental re-thinking, not just fiddling about with the existing pattern of things - often in autocratic and destructive ways. Aptly, into this situation, comes Roland Meighan's book, The Next Learning System. It sets down the reasons for change, the patterns for change, and it hones in on the dynamics of the learning mind."
Dr. James Hemming

ISBN   1-900219-04-2   £7-95

Educational Heretics Press,
113 Arundel Drive, Bramcote Hills, Nottingham NG9 3FQ

Telephone/fax 0115 925 7261

www.gn.apc.org/edheretics

---

and from Education Now at the same address:

Getting Started in Home Education: a handbook

by Mary Ann Rose and Paul Stanbrook

Since taking our own children out of school and embarking on home-based education some five years ago, we have been contacted frequently by parents about to do the same thing or considering this course of action. Their questions include: What do we put in the place of school? What materials and resources are available to parents? Do we need specialist help and, if so, where can we obtain it? Are there other home-based educators nearby who might want to communicate or work with us? How do we deal with the Local Education Authority? Will its officers know much about the learner-managed, autonomous approach favoured by many home-based educators, since their training will have been in the 'crowd instruction' mode? What will home-based education mean for the life of the parents?

ISBN   1-871526-42-6   £17-50

Some useful contacts

Education Otherwise is the largest home-based education self-help group in UK. For information, send an A5 size stamped addressed envelope to:
P.O.Box 7420, London N9 9SG
Helpline: 0870 7300074
www/education-otherwise.org

Home Education Advisory Service (HEAS) provides information, advice and support for home-educating families.
www.heas.org.uk

Herald (Home Education Resources and Learning Development)
Support and study materials for new and experienced home-educating families.
Herald, Kelda Cottage, Lydbrook, GL17 9SX
01594 861107
www.homeeducation.co.uk

Choice in Education, monthly magazine assembled by a team of home-educating volunteers
P.O Box 20284, London NW1 3WY
020 8969 0893
www.choiceineducation.co.uk

See also:
www.home-education.org.uk
www.home-ed.org
www.edheretics.gn.apc.org
www.educationnow.gn.apc.org